The U.S.
Climate Change Science Program

Vision for the Program
and Highlights
of the Scientific Strategic Plan

July 2003

A Report by the Climate Change Science Program and
the Subcommittee on Global Change Research

July 2003

Members of Congress:

Transmitted herewith is a copy of *The U.S. Climate Change Science Program: Vision for the Program and Highlights of the Scientific Strategic Plan*. The vision document provides an overview of the Climate Change Science Program (CCSP) long-term strategic plan to enhance scientific understanding of global climate change. This document is a companion to the comprehensive *Strategic Plan for the Climate Change Science Program*.

The Strategic Plan for the Climate Change Science Program responds to the President's direction that climate change research activities be accelerated to provide the best possible scientific information to support public discussion and decisionmaking on climate-related issues. The plan also responds to Section 104 of the Global Change Research Act of 1990, which mandates the development and periodic updating of a long-term national global change research plan coordinated through the National Science and Technology Council. This is the first comprehensive update of a strategic plan for U.S. global change and climate change research since the original plan for the U.S. Global Change Research Program was adopted at the inception of the program in 1989.

The President established the U.S. Climate Change Science Program in 2002 as part of a new cabinet-level management structure to oversee public investments in climate change science and technology. The new management structure also includes the Climate Change Technology Program, which is responsible for accelerating climate-related technology research and development. The CCSP incorporates the U.S. Global Change Research Program, established by the Global Change Research Act, and the Climate Change Research Initiative, established by the President in 2001. The Program coordinates and integrates scientific research on global change and climate change sponsored by 13 participating departments and agencies of the U.S. Government.

The CCSP, under the direction of the Assistant Secretary of Commerce for Oceans and Atmosphere, reports through the Interagency Working Group on Climate Change Science and Technology to the cabinet-level Committee on Climate Change Science and Technology Integration. The chairmanship of these coordinating bodies rotates annually between the Departments of Commerce and Energy, with the Director of the Office of Science and Technology Policy serving as the Executive Director of the cabinet-level committee.

The CCSP strategic plan, though disseminated by the Department of Commerce, was developed through a multi-agency collaboration and has benefited substantially from external review of an earlier discussion draft by a special committee of the National Academy of Sciences – National Research Council, as well as extensive public review by hundreds of scientists and stakeholders. The strategic plan document contains a more detailed discussion of the goals and priorities for the program and how climate and global change research activities will be integrated.

The CCSP strategic plan reflects a commitment to high-quality research that advances the frontiers of science and outlines an integrated approach for developing an improved understanding of climate change and its potential impacts. The program described in the vision and strategic plan documents will meet the highest standards of credibility and transparency to support public evaluation of climate change issues.

We thank the participating departments and agencies of the CCSP for their close cooperation and support and look forward to working with Congress in the continued development of these important programs.

Spencer Abraham
Secretary of Energy
Chair, Committee on Climate Change
Science and Technology Integration

Donald L. Evans
Secretary of Commerce
Vice Chair, Committee on Climate Change
Science and Technology Integration

John H. Marburger III, Ph.D.
Director, Office of Science and Technology Policy
Executive Director, Committee
on Climate Change
Science and Technology Integration

TABLE OF CONTENTS

OVERVIEW

The Need for the Best Available Science to Address Global Climate Change Issues

"The Earth's well-being is also an issue important to America. And it's an issue that should be important to every nation in every part of our world. The issue of climate change respects no border. Its effects cannot be reined in by an army nor advanced by any ideology. Climate change, with its potential to impact every corner of the world, is an issue that must be addressed by the world."

— President Bush, June 11, 2001

Climate shapes the environment, natural resources, the economy, and other aspects of life in all countries of the world. Natural and human-induced changes in climate, as well as the options suggested for adapting to or slowing changes, may have substantial environmental, economic, and societal consequences. Decisionmakers, resource managers, and other interested citizens need reliable science-based information to make informed judgments regarding policy and actions. Figure 1 illustrates some of the range and complexity of the climate system elements that must be considered in addressing short- and long-term climate change issues.

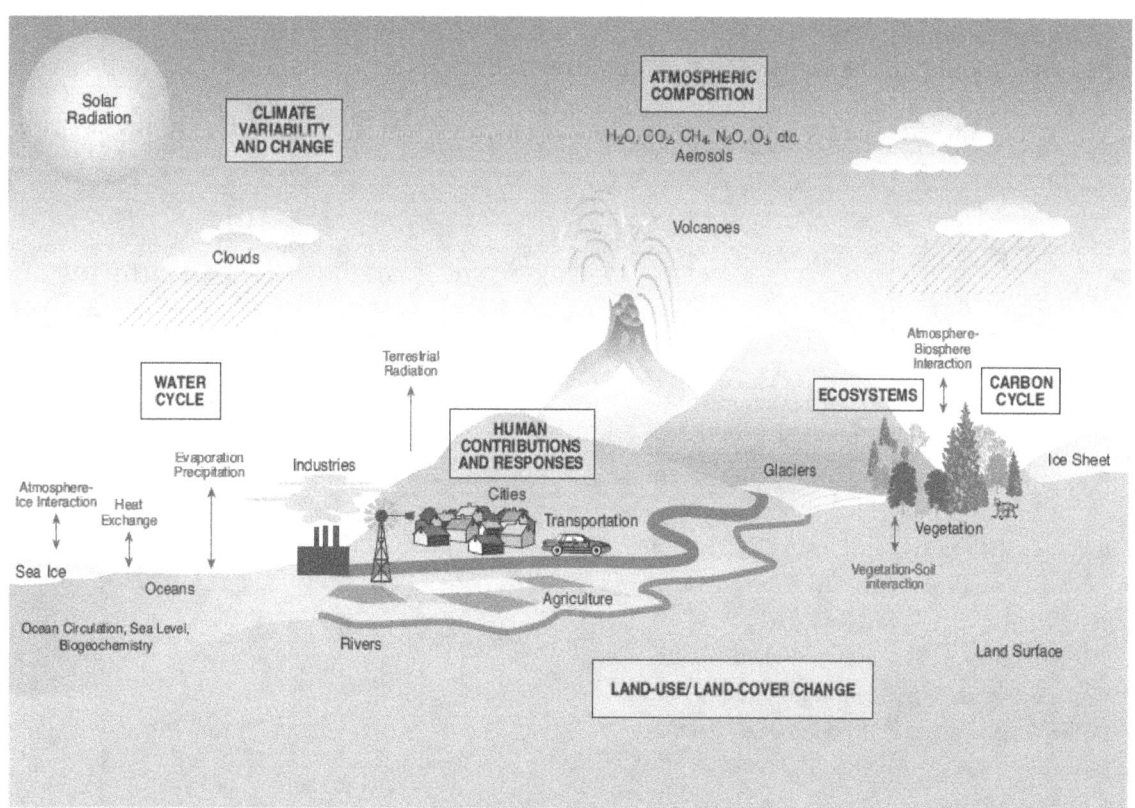

Figure 1: Major components needed to understand the climate system and climate change.

In May 2001, the Administration asked the National Academy of Sciences – National Research Council (NRC) to provide an updated evaluation of key questions about climate change science. Upon receipt of the NRC's report in June 2001, the President directed the relevant agencies and departments of the federal government to build on the extensive U.S. Global Change Research Program (USGCRP) to accelerate research on the most important uncertainties in climate science, enhance climate observation systems, and improve information available to decisionmakers. To accomplish this, the Administration took several steps:

- The President launched the Climate Change Research Initiative (CCRI) in June 2001, with an enhanced focus on the climate effects of aerosols (tiny particles) in the atmosphere, the carbon cycle in the Earth system, climate modeling, observations, and development of scientific information to support decisionmaking.
- The President created a new, cabinet-level organization in February 2002, to improve the government-wide management of climate science and climate-related technology development. Two collaborative interagency programs were launched in response to the President's direction: the Climate Change Science Program (CCSP) and the Climate Change Technology Program (CCTP).
- In July 2002, a year-long process to prepare a 10-year strategic plan for the CCSP was initiated. This planning process was designed to ensure a comprehensive examination of research and observation needs, transparent review by all the international scientific and stakeholder communities, and establishment of defined goals for the research. This document, together with the companion CCSP scientific strategic plan, represents the culmination of the planning and public review process.
- The United States has also launched an international effort to design and implement a comprehensive, multilaterally sponsored Earth observing system, which will provide critical information to improve climate science and modeling. This system will build directly upon

the major advances in observations and data management already achieved by the United States and other nations. A ministerial meeting hosted by the U.S. government in Washington in July 2003 is the first step in a planned 10-year effort to greatly improve the ability to "take the temperature of the Earth."

Vision and Goals

Research and observations can play unique roles in helping society to deal with key climate change issues. This gives rise to the guiding vision of the U.S. Climate Change Science Program.

GUIDING VISION FOR THE CCSP

A nation and the global community empowered with the science-based knowledge to manage the risks and opportunities of change in the climate and related environmental systems.

Five principal goals have been adopted to guide the CCSP.

CCSP GOAL 1

Improve knowledge of the Earth's past and present climate and environment, including its natural variability, and improve understanding of the causes of observed variability and change.

CCSP GOAL 2

Improve quantification of the forces bringing about changes in the Earth's climate and related systems.

CCSP GOAL 3

Reduce uncertainty in projections of how the Earth's climate and related systems may change in the future.

CCSP GOAL 4

Understand the sensitivity and adaptability of different natural and managed ecosystems and human systems to climate and related global changes.

CCSP GOAL 5

Explore the uses and identify the limits of evolving knowledge to manage risks and opportunities related to climate variability and change.

By developing information with the aim of achieving these goals, the program will ensure that it addresses the most important climate-related issues. For each of the goals, the CCSP will prepare science-based information resources that support policy discussions and decisionmaking.

CCSP Priorities

While the CCSP Strategic Plan includes a decade-long strategy, it also establishes priorities for the near term consistent with the President's Climate Change Research Initiative. The program prioritizes three broad sets of scientific uncertainties: atmospheric distributions and effects of aerosols; climate feedbacks and sensitivity, initially focusing on polar feedbacks; and carbon sources and sinks, focusing particularly on North America.

The CCSP will also focus on climate observing systems, including efforts to document historical records, improve observations for use in climate models, enhance ecological observing systems, and improve data and information system architectures.

Development of state-of-the-art climate modeling that will improve understanding of the causes and impacts of climate change is also a CCSP priority. These models will be key assets in helping policymakers, planners, and resource managers address climate change issues.

CCSP Principal Products

The CCSP plan calls for the creation of a series of more than 20 synthesis and assessment reports during the next 4 years. These reports respond to the CCSP highest priority research, observation, and decision support needs.

In addition to the scheduled integrated reports, the CCSP agencies will continue to sponsor a large number of research projects and observation programs each year. The products of these activities – a wide array of peer-reviewed scientific publications and major observation records – are a major continuing legacy of the CCSP.

Development of the Strategic Plan

This Vision Document provides an overview of the CCSP's long-term Strategic Plan to guide the research effort. The Vision Document focuses primarily on the goals, products, and approaches of the CCSP. The Strategic Plan, spanning more than 300-pages, will guide the coordinated efforts of the 13 agencies participating in the CCSP. The Strategic Plan provides more detailed information on the scientific questions and objectives addressed by the program, as well as additional information on the current state of knowledge. The table of contents of the Strategic Plan is reproduced as Appendix A.

The Strategic Plan responds to the President's direction that climate change research activities be accelerated to provide the best possible scientific information needed for climate-related decisions. The plan reflects a commitment to high-quality science, which requires openness to review and critique by the wider scientific and stakeholder communities. The process by which the plan was drafted incorporates the transparency essential for scientific credibility. The program received extensive comments and suggestions during its *Climate Science Workshop* in December 2002 attended by more than 1,300 scientists and other participants, including individuals from 47 states and 36 nations. In the weeks following the workshop, the CCSP also received 270 sets of written public comments, involving nearly 900 pages of text. In addition, the CCSP requested and received a detailed evaluation (released in February 2003) from a special committee of the National Research Council. The NRC will provide a second public report in late 2003, expressing the committee's conclusions and recommendations on the content, objectivity, quality, and comprehensiveness of the updated Strategic Plan, on the open process used to produce it, and on the proposed process for developing subsequent findings to be reported by the CCSP.

The Administration's Actions to Enhance Scientific Understanding of Global Climate Change

"My Cabinet-level working group has met regularly for the last 10 weeks to review the most recent, most accurate, and most comprehensive science. They have heard from scientists offering a wide spectrum of views. They have reviewed the facts, and they have listened to many theories and suppositions. The working group asked the highly respected National Academy of Sciences to provide us the most up-to-date information about what is known and about what is not known on the science of climate change."

—President Bush, June 11, 2001

Scientific Review Requested from the National Academy of Sciences

In May 2001, the Administration asked the National Academy of Sciences' National Research Council to provide an updated evaluation of key questions about climate change science, with reference to the recently completed *Third Assessment Report* of the Intergovernmental Panel on Climate Change (IPCC), and with reference to ongoing climate change research in the United States and other nations. The NRC committee report, *Climate Change Science: An Analysis of Some Key Questions,* was issued in June 2001. The summary of the report stated:

"Greenhouse gases are accumulating in Earth's atmosphere as a result of human activities, causing surface air temperatures and subsurface ocean temperatures to rise. Temperatures are, in fact, rising. The changes observed over the last several decades are likely mostly due to human activities, but we cannot rule out that some significant part of these changes is also a reflection of natural variability. Human-induced warming and associated sea level rises are expected to continue through the 21st century...Because there is considerable uncertainty in current understanding of how the climate system varies naturally and reacts to emissions of greenhouse gases and aerosols, current estimates of the magnitude of future warming should be regarded as tentative and subject to future adjustments (either upward or downward)...

"Making progress in reducing the large uncertainties in projections of future climate will require addressing a number of fundamental scientific questions relating to the buildup of greenhouse gases in the atmosphere and the behavior of the climate system...In addition, the research enterprise dealing with environmental change and the interactions of human society with the environment must be enhanced...An effective strategy for advancing the understanding of climate change also will require (1) a global observing system in support of long-term climate monitoring and prediction, (2) concentration on large-scale modeling through increased, dedicated supercomputing and human resources, and (3) efforts to ensure that climate research is supported and managed to ensure innovation, effectiveness, and efficiency."

The key areas addressed in the June 2001 NRC report include climate observations; the influence of aerosols in the atmosphere; carbon sources and sinks in the atmosphere, oceans, and ecosystems; climate modeling; scenarios of human-induced climate impacts; and the integration of scientific knowledge, including its uncertainty, into effective decision support systems. These considerations have guided the development of the focused climate research and technology initiatives announced by the President that same month.

The Climate Change Research Initiative Launched in June 2001

"As we analyze the possibilities, we will be guided by several basic principles. Our approach must be consistent with the long-term goal of stabilizing greenhouse gas concentrations in the atmosphere. Our actions should be measured as we learn more from science and build on it…We will act, learn, and act again, adjusting our approaches as science advances and technology evolves. Our administration will be creative."

—*President Bush, June 11, 2001*

Upon receipt of the NRC report in June 2001, the President launched the U.S. Climate Change Research Initiative "…to study areas of uncertainty and identify priority areas where investments can make a difference." The CCRI represents a focusing of resources and attention on those elements of the USGCRP that can best support improved public debate and decisionmaking in the near term. The goal of the CCRI is to improve integration of scientific knowledge (including measures of uncertainty) into policy and management decisions and evaluation of management strategies and choices—within the next 5 years.

To meet this goal, and consistent with the National Research Council reports, the CCRI aims to:

1. Reduce scientific uncertainty in three key areas of climate science:

Develop reliable representations of the climatic forcing resulting from atmospheric aerosols. Aerosols and tropospheric ozone play unique, but poorly quantified, roles in the atmospheric radiation budget. Proposed activities include field campaigns (including aircraft missions), *in situ* monitoring stations, improved modeling, and satellite data algorithm development.

Improve our understanding of the global carbon cycle (sources and sinks). CCRI funds will be targeted for activities to carry out the integrated North American Carbon Program (NACP), a key element of the U.S. Carbon Cycle Science Plan. This program will improve monitoring techniques, reconcile approaches for quantifying carbon storage, and elucidate key processes and land management practices regulating carbon fluxes between the atmosphere and the land and ocean.

Increase our knowledge of climate feedback processes. Poor understanding of "climate feedbacks"—key interactions among two or more components of the climate system, such as clouds, water vapor, ocean circulation, or sea ice—are responsible for large uncertainties in our ability to reliably predict climate variability and change. CCRI will prioritize activities to support increased understanding of feedback processes.

2. Enhance and expand observations of the Earth system. CCRI efforts will contribute to and benefit from the design and operational implementation over the next 10 years of a new international, integrated, sustained, and comprehensive global Earth observation system to minimize data gaps and maximize the utility of existing observing networks.

3. Increase our climate modeling capacity.

CCRI will support continued development and refinement of computational climate models. Priority activities will focus on improving model physics (particularly with respect to clouds and aerosols), increasing resolution of climate model simulations, improving methods to assimilate observations into model analyses and predictions, and exploring limits to predictability of climate variability and change. CCRI will also support development of climate modeling to provide routine model products for policy and management decision support.

The President also launched the parallel Climate Change Technology Program in June 2001, "…to strengthen research at universities and national labs, to enhance partnerships in applied research, to develop improved technology for measuring and monitoring gross and net greenhouse gas emissions, and to fund demonstration projects for cutting-edge technologies." Technological breakthroughs will be needed to address the long-term challenge of global climate change. The CCSP and the CCTP are closely collaborating to ensure that: (a) science drives the definition of technology needs; and (b) science is used to evaluate the potential consequences of proposed technology innovations.

Integration of the Short-Term CCRI and the Long-Term USGCRP to Form The Climate Change Science Program

The Administration's Climate Change Research Initiative is accelerating key areas of long-term research supported by the U.S. Global Change Research Program. The USGCRP was established by the Global Change Research Act of 1990 to address natural and human-induced changes in the Earth's global environmental system; to monitor, understand, and predict global change; and to provide a sound scientific basis for national and international decisionmaking. To date, more than $20 billion of research funding has supported the USGCRP.

The near-term focus of the CCRI on key climate change uncertainties is being balanced with the breadth of the long-term USGCRP, creating the combined CCSP program that accelerates research on key science uncertainties while supporting long-term advances in understanding the physical, biological, and chemical processes that influence the Earth system. The budgets of the CCRI and USGCRP program elements are developed and maintained separately within the Climate Change Science Program, but the program management structure is identical for both the CCRI and USGCRP elements. This combined management focus is consistent with the recommendations of the 1999 report of the National Research Council, *Global Environmental Change: Research Pathways for the Next Decade.* The *Pathways* report formulated a framework of research questions that has significantly influenced the development of the CCSP Strategic Plan.

The CCSP must also integrate the products of capabilities that make essential contributions to global change research, but were outside the original USGCRP framework. These include the operational environmental satellite system, various *in situ* ocean and atmospheric observing systems, and associated data centers. This will facilitate the transition of research observations into operational systems and the use of research products by mission agencies.

New Cabinet-Level Management Structure Created in February 2002 to Oversee the Climate Change Science Program and the Climate Change Technology Program

In February 2002, the President created a new Cabinet-level management structure, the Committee on Climate Change Science and Technology Integration, to oversee the more than $3 billion annual investment in the combined federal climate change research and technology development programs. The new management structure places accountability and leadership for the science and technology programs in the relevant cabinet departments (see Figure 2). The relevant research continues to be coordinated through the National Science and Technology Council in accordance with the Global Change Research Act of 1990.

Under the new management structure, the CCSP integrates research on global climate change sponsored by the Departments of Agriculture, Commerce, Defense, Energy, Health and Human Services, the Interior, State, and Transportation,

together with the Environmental Protection Agency, the National Aeronautics and Space Administration, the National Science Foundation, the Agency for International Development, and the Smithsonian Institution. The Office of Science and Technology Policy, the Council on Environmental Quality, the National Economic Council, and the Office of Management and Budget also participate. The principal areas of global change research for the CCSP agencies are summarized in Appendix B.

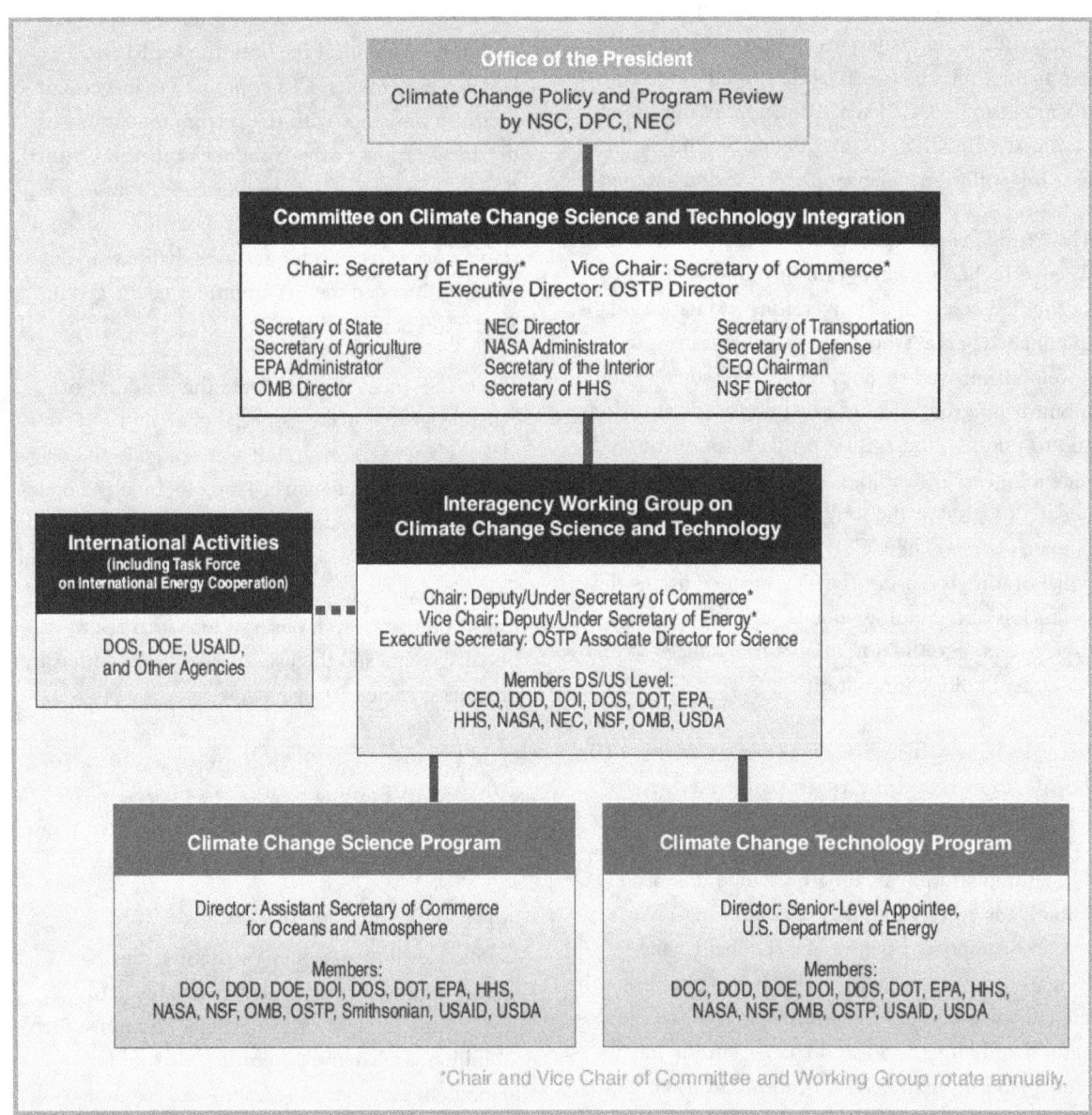

Figure 2: Climate science and technology management structure.

Development of the CCSP Strategic Plan

"A fully updated strategic plan for U.S. global change research is under development. This will be the first comprehensive update to the strategic plan for the USGCRP (and CCRI) since the original plan was adopted."

—Secretary of Commerce Donald L. Evans and Secretary of Energy Spencer Abraham
Letter to the President, September 9, 2002

The CCSP Strategic Plan responds to the President's direction that climate change research activities be accelerated to provide the best possible scientific information needed for climate-related decisions. The plan reflects a commitment to high-quality science, which requires openness to review and critique by the wider scientific and stakeholder communities. The process by which the Plan was drafted incorporates the transparency essential for scientific credibility.

The Administration released the CCSP *Discussion Draft Strategic Plan* for public review in November 2002. The discussion draft built upon the significant investments already made in climate change science, and was guided by the priority information needs identified by scientists and stakeholders (i.e., individuals or groups whose interests— financial, cultural, value-based, or other—are affected by climate variability, climate change, or options for adapting to or mitigating these phenomena), both nationally and internationally. It outlined a comprehensive, collaborative approach for developing a more accurate understanding of climate change and its potential impacts.

External comments played an important role in revising the initial draft of the plan. A *Climate Change Science Program Workshop* held in December 2002 in Washington, DC, was attended by 1,300 scientists and other participants, including individuals from 47 states and 36 nations. The workshop was designed to facilitate extensive discussion and comments on the draft plan from all interested domestic and international groups and individuals,

including the scientific community, stakeholders, non-governmental organizations, interested members of the public, and the media.

Written comments on the *Discussion Draft Strategic Plan* were submitted during a public review period. When collated, these comments amounted to nearly 900 pages of input from hundreds of scientists, representatives of interest groups, and interested members of the lay public.

In addition, a special committee of the National Academy of Sciences' National Research Council reviewed the plan at the request of the CCSP. The special 17-member review committee included experts in the physical, biological, social, and economic sciences. In February 2003, this committee reported its recommendations, which have provided invaluable assistance in the revision of the draft plan. The NRC committee will provide a second public report in late 2003, expressing the committee's conclusions and recommendations on the content, objectivity, quality, and comprehensiveness of the updated Strategic Plan, on the open process used to produce it, and on the proposed process for developing subsequent findings to be reported by the CCSP.

The CCSP Strategic Plan is being published after consideration of all of the workshop discussions, the full range of written public review comments received by January 2003, and the NRC review of the discussion draft plan, as well as an extensive internal U.S. Government review process.

The plan will guide the conduct of research activities sponsored or conducted by the U.S. Government. It will be modified as warranted by the emergence of key findings and important new public questions.

After the release of the Strategic Plan, the CCSP will serve in a "credible fact finder" capacity—providing a source of reliable and useful information to support decisions on global climate change issues. It will focus on developing synthesis and assessment reports on climate science findings. Future reports will address the principal foci of the Strategic Plan, which are (a) reducing key scientific uncertainties, (b) designing and implementing a comprehensive global climate and ecosystem monitoring and data management system, and (c) providing information (from a range of scenarios and response options) that supports public evaluation of climate change response options.

The United States is a world leader in climate change research, investing more than $20 billion on such research in the past 12 years. Even with substantial budgets, the potential scope of climate change research, observations, and scientific synthesis is so large that the CCSP must clearly identify the highest priority activities for support. This section outlines the high-priority CCSP topics and the basis for their designation. The overall criteria used to guide individual program and project support decisions are also described.

Information Sources for Determining High-Priority Activities

In developing priorities, the CCSP has considered information from many sources, including:

- The analysis and reporting requirements imposed by the Global Change Research Act of 1990 (Public Law 101–606)
- The focus on reducing key scientific uncertainties through the Climate Change Research Initiative of June 2001
- The recommendations in various reports of the National Research Council, including the following key NRC reports:
  - *Climate Change Science: An Analysis of Some Key Questions,* requested by the Administration and published in June 2001
  - *Global Environmental Change: Research Pathways for the Next Decade*, a seminal report published in 1999
  - *Planning Climate and Global Change Research*, requested by the Administration as part of the CCSP Strategic Plan development and published in February 2003
- Climate change assessment reports by the Intergovernmental Panel on Climate Change
- The annual program plans of the 13 collaborating CCSP agencies and departments, as documented in the annual series of *Our Changing Planet* reports

- The *Discussion Draft Strategic Plan* published by the CCSP in November 2002
- The deliberations at the *Climate Change Science Workshop* in December 2002, which was sponsored by the CCSP and attended by 1,300 climate specialists
- The written comments submitted after the December 2002 CCSP workshop.

Priorities Related to Reducing Key Uncertainties as Recommended by the NRC

The June 2001 NRC report requested by the Administration provides an extensive summary of key climate uncertainties to be addressed. The President's June 2001 CCRI initiative took special note of these NRC recommendations, and directed that additional investments be directed to address these important knowledge gaps. More detailed information from the NRC report appears in Appendix C, and key research priorities identified by the NRC follow:

"Predictions of global climate change will require major advances in understanding and modeling of (1) the factors that determine atmospheric concentrations of greenhouse gases and aerosols, and (2) the so-called "feedbacks" that determine the sensitivity of the climate system to a prescribed increase in greenhouse gases. Specifically, this will involve reducing uncertainty regarding: (a) future usage of fossil fuels, (b) future emissions of methane, (c) the fraction of the future fossil fuel carbon that will remain in the atmosphere and provide radiative forcing versus exchange with the oceans or net exchange with the land biosphere, (d) the feedbacks in the climate system that determine both the magnitude of the change and the rate of energy uptake by the oceans, which together determine the

ATMOSPHERIC COMPOSITION
CLIMATE VARIABILITY AND CHANGE
GLOBAL WATER CYCLE
LAND-USE/LAND-COVER CHANGE
GLOBAL CARBON CYCLE
ECOSYSTEMS
HUMAN CONTRIBUTIONS AND RESPONSES

Atmospheric Composition

The atmosphere is a protective envelope for life on Earth, providing key ingredients necessary to sustain life and shielding the planet from harmful radiation. It can transport materials around the globe in a matter of weeks yet can hold chemicals for centuries or longer. The concentrations of the key gases that might affect climate are changing, as are the processes that affect the composition of the atmosphere.

CCSP-supported research focuses on how human activities and natural processes alter the composition of the atmosphere and its energy balance and how related changes could influence climate, ozone, ultraviolet radiation, pollutant exposure, ecosystems, and human health. Specific objectives address the recovery of the stratospheric ozone layer; the properties and distributions of greenhouse gases and aerosols; long-range transport of chemicals and aerosols and implications for regional air quality; and integrated assessments of the effects of these changes. Issues involving interactions between atmospheric composition and climate are of particular interest.

Benefits from this research include:
• Improved description of the global distributions of aerosols and their radiative properties
• Knowledge of the importance of other greenhouse gases besides carbon dioxide in the climate system

• Understanding the recovery of the ozone layer (resulting from international compliance with the Montreal Protocol on Substances that Deplete the Ozone Layer) and its relationship with the climate system

• Strengthened processes within the national and international scientific communities to provide for integrated evaluation of impacts from air pollution and changes in climate on ecosystems and human health.

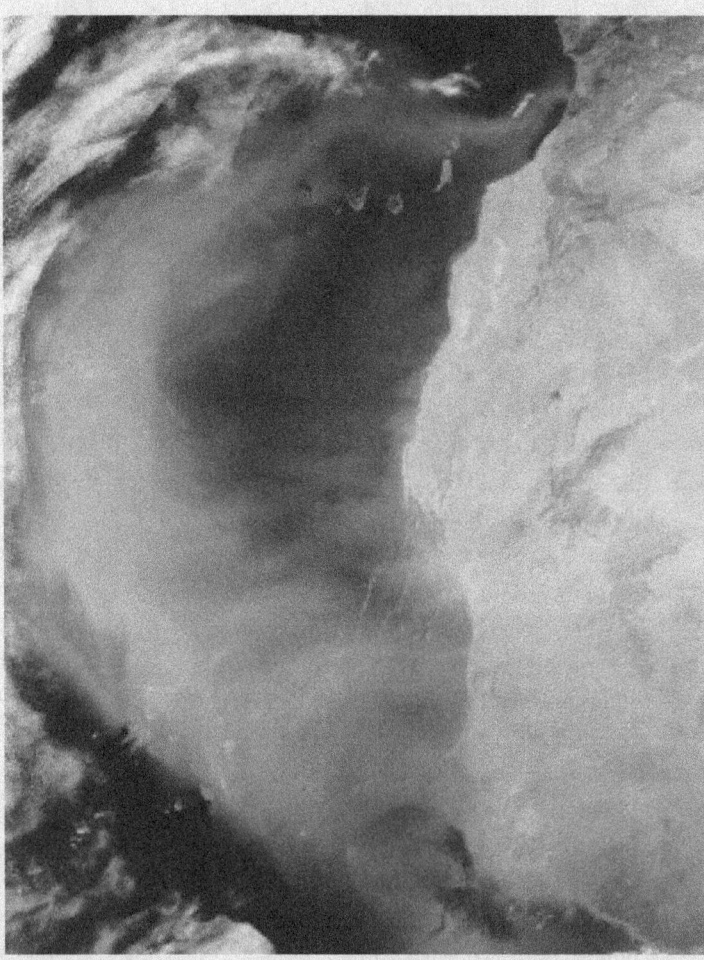

Saharan Dust Off West Africa. The plume extends more than 1,000 miles (1,600 km). Scientists are trying to fully understand how such tiny airborne particles — emitted worldwide from many different sources — affect climate.

magnitude and time history of the temperature increases for a given radiative forcing, (e) the details of the regional and local climate change consequent to an overall level of global climate change, (f) the nature and causes of the natural variability of climate and its interactions with forced changes, and (g) the direct and indirect effects of the changing distributions of aerosol. Because the total change in radiative forcing from other greenhouse gases over the last century has been nearly as large as that of carbon dioxide, their future evolution also must be addressed. At the heart of this is basic research, which allows for creative discoveries about those elements of the climate system that have not yet been identified, or studied.

"Knowledge of the climate system and projections about the future climate are derived from fundamental physics and chemistry through models and observations of the atmosphere and the climate system. Climate models are built using the best scientific knowledge of the processes that operate within the climate system, which in turn are based on observations of these systems. A major limitation of these model forecasts for use around the world is the paucity of data available to evaluate the ability of coupled models to simulate important aspects of past climate. In addition, the observing system available today is a composite of observations that neither provides the information nor the continuity in the data needed to support measurements of climate variables. Therefore, above all, it is essential to ensure the existence of a long-term observing system that provides a more definitive observational foundation to evaluate decadal- to century-scale variability and change. This observing system must include observations of key state variables such as temperature, precipitation, humidity, pressure, clouds, sea ice and snow cover, sea level, sea-surface temperature, carbon fluxes, and soil moisture. Additionally, more comprehensive regional measurements of greenhouse gases would provide critical information about their local and regional source strengths.

"Climate observations and modeling are becoming increasingly important for a wide segment of society including water resource managers, public health officials, agribusinesses, energy providers, forest managers, insurance companies, and city planners. In order to address the consequences of climate change and better serve the nation's decisionmakers, the research enterprise dealing with environmental change and environment-society interactions must be enhanced. This includes support of (a) interdisciplinary research that couples physical, chemical, biological, and human systems, (b) improved capability [to] integrate scientific knowledge, including its uncertainty, into effective decision support systems, and (c) an ability to conduct research at the regional or sectoral level that promotes analysis of the response of human and natural systems to multiple stresses."

CCSP Responses to the Identified Priority Research Needs

The research priorities of the CCSP are reviewed on an annual cycle through the budget process and reflect priority needs and scientific opportunities. While the CCSP Strategic Plan includes a decade-long strategy, it also establishes priorities for the near term consistent with the CCRI. These priorities have been established in response to information from the above sources. These priorities are reflected in a focusing of resources and enhanced interagency coordination of ongoing and planned research that can best address major gaps in understanding of climate change. The CCSP Strategic Plan provides additional information on these priorities.

For the near term, the CCSP will emphasize research on three sets of scientific uncertainties highlighted by the NRC: (1) atmospheric distributions and effects of aerosols; (2) climate feedbacks and sensitivity, initially focusing on polar feedbacks; and (3) carbon sources and sinks, focusing particularly on North America.

ATMOSPHERIC COMPOSITION
CLIMATE VARIABILITY AND CHANGE
GLOBAL WATER CYCLE
LAND-USE/LAND-COVER CHANGE
GLOBAL CARBON CYCLE
ECOSYSTEMS
HUMAN CONTRIBUTIONS AND RESPONSES

Climate Variability and Change

Climate and climate variability influence social and natural environments throughout the world. Climate fluctuations on various time scales affect the success of agriculture, the abundance and distribution of water, and the demand for energy. Human-induced changes in climate may have substantial environmental, economic, and societal consequences.

CCSP-supported research on climate variability and change focuses on how climate elements such as temperature, precipitation, clouds, winds, and storminess are affected by changes in the Earth that result from natural processes and potentially human activities. Specific objectives include: improved predictions of seasonal to decadal climate variations (e.g., the El Niño-Southern Oscillation); improved detection, attribution, and projections of longer term changes in climate; the potential for changes in extreme events; the possibility of abrupt climate change; and efficient and effective methods of disseminating accurate and useful scientific information about climate needed for decisions.

Benefits from this research include:
• Improved ability to distinguish natural climatic variations from human contributions to climate change, resulting in more credible answers to "If…, then…" policy-related questions

• Improved forecasts of El Niño events
• Better estimates of future changes in extreme events and of risks of abrupt changes
• Improved communication and increased use of scientific information on climate variability and change.

In Situ Measurements. This surface buoy with meteorological instrumentation is being deployed in the Arabian Sea to help researchers study surface forcings. Source: Robert A. Weller, Woods Hole Oceanographic Institution.

The CCSP will also focus on climate observing systems including efforts to: (a) document historical records; (b) improve observations for model development and applications; (c) enhance biological and ecological observing systems; and (d) improve data archiving and information system architectures. These activities will involve substantial collaboration with the international climate science community and with several ongoing international programs. The CCSP observation and data management activities will support a major international initiative to develop a comprehensive, integrated Earth observing system. This 10-year international initiative is being launched at an Earth Observation Summit hosted by the United States in July 2003 in Washington, DC. Development of state-of-the-art climate modeling that will improve understanding of the causes and impacts of climate change is also a CCSP priority. Based on recommendations in several NRC reports on U.S. climate modeling and USGCRP evaluations, the CCSP agencies are prioritizing new activities to strengthen U.S. national climate modeling infrastructure.

Finally, the CCSP plan calls for the creation of a series of more than 20 synthesis and assessment reports during the next 4 years. These reports represent principal responses to the top-priority research, observation, and decision support needs described above. The following section describes these reports in the context of the five overarching goals for CCSP.

In addition to the planned synthesis and assessment reports, the CCSP collaborating agencies will continue to sponsor a large number of research projects each year. Prioritization principles also are applied to the entire group of projects in each of the CCSP study areas.

CCSP Criteria for Prioritizing Research, Observations, and Scientific Synthesis Projects

To ensure that the program evolves in response to identified needs, the CCSP has developed the following criteria to assist in reviewing priorities for work elements selected for support:

Scientific or technical quality
- The proposed work must be scientifically rigorous as determined by peer review.
- Implementation plans will include periodic review by external advisory groups (both researchers and users).

Relevance to reducing scientific uncertainties and improving decision support tools in priority areas
- Programs must substantially address one or more of the CCSP goals.
- Programs must respond to needs for scientific information and enhance informed discussion by all relevant stakeholders.

Track record of consistently good past performance and identified metrics for evaluating future progress
- Programs addressing priorities with good track records of past performance will be favored for continued investment to the extent that time tables and metrics for evaluating future progress are provided.
- Proposed programs that identify clear milestones for periodic assessment and documentation of progress will be favorably considered for new investment.

Cost and value
- Research should address CCSP goals in a cost-effective way.
- Research should be coordinated with and leverage other national and international efforts.
- Programs that provide value-added products to improve decision support resources will be favored.

ATMOSPHERIC COMPOSITION
CLIMATE VARIABILITY AND CHANGE
GLOBAL WATER CYCLE
LAND-USE/LAND-COVER CHANGE
GLOBAL CARBON CYCLE
ECOSYSTEMS
HUMAN CONTRIBUTIONS AND RESPONSES

Global Water Cycle

Water is crucial to life on Earth. Water changes from solid to liquid to gas through a natural cycle that also transports and converts energy. Changes in water vapor, clouds, high-latitude ice and snow conditions, and land surfaces are important climate feedbacks. Humans depend on predictions of precipitation, evaporation, flow, storage, and extremes (such as floods and droughts) to plan their access to and use of water.

CCSP-supported research on the global water cycle focuses on how natural processes and human activities influence the distribution and quality of water, on whether changes in the water cycle are predictable, and on how variability and change in the water cycle affect society. Specific areas include: identifying fluctuations of the water cycle and determining the causes of these changes; predicting precipitation and evaporation on time scales of months to years and longer; and modeling various physical, biological, and socioeconomic processes to facilitate efficient water resources management.

Benefits from these research efforts include:

- Measurably improved forecasts of precipitation and other water cycle variables for water managers
- Enhanced ability to incorporate cloud feedbacks and precipitation processes in climate models
- Long-term global and regional data sets of critical water-cycle variables from satellite and surface-based observations, helping to monitor climate trends and promptly detect climate change
- Increases in the efficiency of water use through better water models for policy and planning.

The Aqua Satellite. Launched into space in May 2002, NASA's Earth Observing System (EOS) satellite Aqua generates data on the water cycle and other aspects of the environment. Source: NASA.

CCSP Goals

The CCSP has adopted five overarching scientific goals. By developing information responsive to these goals, the program will ensure that it addresses the most important climate-related issues. For each of the goals, the CCSP will prepare information resources that support climate-related discussions and decisions. These will include scientific synthesis and assessment analyses that support evaluation of important policy issues. A table for each goal identifies the initial topics to be addressed by these products.

GOAL 1

Improve knowledge of the Earth's past and present climate and environment, including its natural variability, and improve understanding of the causes of observed variability and change.

Climate conditions change significantly over the span of seasons, years, decades, and even longer time scales. CCSP research will improve useful understanding of natural climate cycles on timescales from seasons to centuries. Research will include improving forecasts of the El Niño-Southern Oscillation (ENSO)—a large-scale climate cycle (of approximately 2-year duration) with implications for resource management—as well as other natural climate cycles. The program also will expand observations, monitoring, and data/information system capabilities and increase confidence in our understanding of how and why climate is changing. Fostering the transition of research observations to long-term operational measurements and activities will be important.

Specific research foci addressing this goal are:
- Better understand the natural long-term cycles in climate (e.g., Pacific Decadal Variability, North Atlantic Oscillation)
- Improve and harness the capability to forecast El Niño-La Niña events and other seasonal to interannual cycles of variability
- Sharpen understanding of climate extremes through improved observations, analyses, and modeling, and determine whether any changes in their frequency or intensity lie outside the range of natural variability
- Increase confidence in the understanding of how and why climate has changed
- Expand observations and data/information system capabilities.

TOPICS FOR PRIORITY CCSP SYNTHESIS PRODUCTS	SIGNIFICANCE	COMPLETION
Temperature trends in the lower atmosphere—steps for understanding and reconciling differences.	Inconsistencies in the temperature profiles of different data sets reduce confidence in understanding of how and why climate has changed.	within 2 years
Past climate variability and change in the Arctic and at high latitudes.	High latitudes are especially sensitive and may provide early indications of climate change; new paleoclimate data will provide long-term context for recent observed temperature increases.	within 2 years
Reanalyses of historical climate data for key atmospheric features. Implications for attribution of causes of observed change.	Understanding the magnitude of past climate variations is key to increasing confidence in the understanding of how and why climate has changed and why it may change in the future.	2-4 years

GOAL 2

Improve quantification of the forces bringing about changes in the Earth's climate and related systems.

Combustion of fossil fuels, changes in land cover and land use, and industrial activities produce greenhouse gases, aerosols, and aerosol precursors that alter the composition of the atmosphere and important physical and biological properties of the Earth's surface. These changes have several important climate effects, some of which can be quantified only poorly at present.

Research conducted through the CCSP will reduce uncertainty about the sources and sinks of greenhouse gases and aerosols. It also will reduce the uncertainty regarding climate interactions with ozone in the upper and lower layers of the atmosphere, movement of chemicals and particles in the atmosphere, and regional-scale air quality. Research will improve quantification of the interactions among the carbon cycle, other biological and ecological processes, and land cover and land use to better project atmospheric concentrations of greenhouse gases and support improved decisionmaking. The program also will improve capabilities for developing and analyzing emissions scenarios, in cooperation with the Climate Change Technology Program.

Five research foci support this goal:
- Reduce uncertainty about the sources and sinks of greenhouse gases, emissions of aerosols and their precursors, and their climate effects
- Monitor recovery of the ozone layer and improve understanding of the interactions among climate change, ozone depletion, and other atmospheric processes
- Increase knowledge of the interactions among pollutant emissions, long-range atmospheric transport, climate change, and air quality management
- Develop information on the carbon cycle, land cover and use, and biological/ecological processes by helping to quantify net emissions of carbon dioxide, methane, and other greenhouse gases, thereby improving the evaluation of carbon sequestration strategies and alternative response options
- Improve capabilities to develop and apply emissions and related scenarios for conducting "If…, then…" analyses in cooperation with the CCTP.

TOPICS FOR PRIORITY CCSP SYNTHESIS PRODUCTS	SIGNIFICANCE	COMPLETION
Updating scenarios of greenhouse gas emissions and concentrations, in collaboration with the CCTP. Review of integrated scenario development and application.	Sound, comprehensive emissions scenarios are essential for comparative analysis of how climate may change in the future, as well as for analyses of mitigation and adaptation options.	within 2 years
North American carbon budget and implications for the global carbon cycle.	The buildup of CO_2 and methane in the atmosphere and the fraction of carbon being taken up by North America's ecosystems and coastal oceans are key factors in estimating future climate change.	within 2 years
Aerosol properties and their impacts on climate.	There is a high level of uncertainty about how climate may be affected by different types of aerosols, both warming and cooling, and thus how climate change might be affected by their control.	2-4 years
Trends in emissions of ozone-depleting substances, ozone layer recovery, and implications for ultraviolet radiation exposure and climate change.	This information is key to ensuring that international agreements to phase out production of ozone-depleting substances are having the expected outcome (recovery of the protective ozone layer).	2-4 years

GOAL 3

Reduce uncertainty in projections of how the Earth's climate and related systems may change in the future.

While much is known about the mechanisms that affect the response of the climate system to changes in natural and human influences, significant uncertainty exists as to how much climate will change overall and how it will change in specific regions.

A primary CCSP objective is the development of the information and scientific capacity needed to sharpen qualitative and quantitative understanding through interconnected observations, data assimilation, and modeling activities. Comprehensive climate system models integrate scientific understanding of the many components of the climate system and, thus, are the principal tools available for making quantitative projections.

CCSP-supported research will address not only basic climate system properties and interactions, but also a number of "feedbacks," or secondary changes that can either reinforce or dampen the initial effects of greenhouse gas and aerosol emissions or changes in land use and land cover. The program also will address the potential for changes in the frequency and intensity of extreme events, and will seek to reduce uncertainty regarding potential rapid or discontinuous changes in

climate. The CCSP will build on existing U.S. strengths in climate research and modeling and will help develop "high-end" models that couple the climate with other important physical and biological components of the Earth system.

Research from the program will be integrated to focus on each of these areas:

- Improve characterization of the circulation of the atmosphere and oceans and their interactions through fluxes of energy and materials
- Improve understanding of key "feedbacks" including changes in the amount and distribution of water vapor, extent of ice and the Earth's reflectivity, cloud properties, and biological and ecological systems
- Increase understanding of the conditions that could give rise to events such as rapid changes in ocean circulation owing to changes in temperature and salinity gradients
- Accelerate incorporation of improved knowledge of climate processes and feedbacks into climate models to reduce uncertainty about climate sensitivity (i.e., response to radiative forcing), projected climate changes, and other related conditions
- Improve national capacity to develop and apply climate models.

TOPICS FOR PRIORITY CCSP SYNTHESIS PRODUCTS	SIGNIFICANCE	COMPLETION
Climate models and their uses and limitations, including sensitivity, feedbacks, and uncertainty analysis.	Clarifying the uses and limitations of climate models at different spatial and temporal scales will contribute to appropriate application of these results.	within 2 years
Climate projections for research and assessment based on emissions scenarios developed through the CCTP.	Production of these projections will help develop modeling capacity and will provide important inputs to comparative analysis of response options.	2-4 years
Climate extremes including documentation of current extremes. Prospects for improving projections.	Extreme events have important implications for natural resources, property, infrastructure, and public safety.	2-4 years
Risks of abrupt changes in global climate.	Abrupt changes have occurred in the past and thus it is important to evaluate what we know about the potential for abrupt change in the future.	2-4 years

GOAL 4

Understand the sensitivity and adaptability of different natural and managed ecosystems and human systems to climate and related global changes.

Seasonal to interannual variability in climate has been connected to impacts on almost every aspect of human life. Long time scale natural climate cycles and human-induced changes in climate may have additional effects. Improving the ability to assess potential implications of variations and future changes in climate and environmental conditions could enable governments, businesses, and communities to reduce potential negative impacts and to take advantage of opportunities by adapting infrastructure, activities, and plans.

CCSP research will examine the potential for multiple interacting effects (e.g., the carbon dioxide "fertilization effect," deposition of nitrogen and other nutrients, landscape changes that affect water resources and habitats, changes in frequency of fires or pests) in order to improve knowledge of sensitivity and adaptability to climate variability and change. CCSP research also will improve methods to advance our understanding of the potential effects of different atmospheric concentrations of greenhouse gases and to develop methods for comparing the potential impacts across different sectors.

Research focus areas are:
- Improve knowledge of the sensitivity of ecosystems and economic sectors to global climate variability and change
- Identify and provide scientific inputs for evaluating adaptation options, in cooperation with mission-oriented agencies and other resource managers
- Improve understanding of how changes in ecosystems (including managed ecosystems such as croplands) and human infrastructure interact over long periods of time.

TOPICS FOR PRIORITY CCSP SYNTHESIS PRODUCTS	SIGNIFICANCE	COMPLETION
Coastal elevation and sensitivity to sea level rise.	Evaluation of how well equipped society is to cope with potential sea level rise can help reduce vulnerability.	within 2 years
State-of-knowledge of thresholds of change that could lead to discontinuities (sudden changes) in some ecosystems and climate-sensitive resources.	This approach seeks to determine how much climate change natural environments and resources can withstand before being adversely affected.	2-4 years
Relationship between observed ecosystem changes and climate change.	Earlier blossoming times, longer growing seasons, and other changes are being observed, and this report will explore what is known about why these events are happening.	2-4 years
Preliminary review of adaptation options for climate-sensitive ecosystems and resources.	Understanding of adaptation options can support improved resource management—whether change results from natural or human causes—and thus helps realize opportunities or reduce negative impacts.	2-4 years
Scenario-based analysis of the climatological, environmental, resource, technological, and economic implications of different atmospheric concentrations of greenhouse gases.	Knowing how well we can differentiate the impacts of different greenhouse gas concentrations is important in determining the range of appropriate response policies.	2-4 years
State-of-the-science of socioeconomic and environmental impacts of climate variability.	This product will help improve application of evolving ENSO forecasts by synthesizing information on impacts, both positive and negative, of variability.	2-4 years
Within the transportation sector, a summary of climate change and variability sensitivities, potential impacts, and response options.	Safety and efficiency of transportation infrastructure—much of which has a long lifetime—may be increased through planning that takes account of sensitivities to climate variability and change.	2-4 years

GOAL 5

Explore the uses and identify the limits of evolving knowledge to manage risks and opportunities related to climate variability and change.

Over the last decade, the scientific and technical community has developed a variety of products to support management of risks and opportunities related to climate variability and change. These products have evoked much commentary, both positive and negative. The CCSP will encourage evaluation and learning from these experiences in order to structure decision support processes and products that use scientific knowledge to the best effect, while respecting and disclosing the limits of this knowledge.

The CCSP will develop resources (e.g., observations, databases, data and model products, scenarios, visualization products, scientific syntheses, and assessments) to support policies, planning, and adaptive management. In coordination with the CCTP, the CCSP also will develop and apply frameworks and methods to integrate the complex array of research on human activities, technology, emissions, land-use and land-cover change, nutrient cycles, climatic feedbacks and responses, and potential impacts on ecosystems, resources, and the economy.

Research to explore the uses and identify the limits of evolving knowledge will focus on the following areas:

- Support informed public discussion of issues of particular importance to U.S. decisions by conducting research and providing scientific synthesis and assessment reports
- Support adaptive management and planning for resources and physical infrastructure affected by climate variability and change; build new partnerships with public and private sector entities that can benefit both research and decisions
- Support policymaking by conducting comparative analyses and evaluations of the socioeconomic and environmental consequences of response options.

TOPICS FOR PRIORITY CCSP SYNTHESIS PRODUCTS	SIGNIFICANCE	COMPLETION
Uses and limitations of observations, data, forecasts, and other projections in decision support for selected sectors and regions.	There is a great need for regional climate information; further evaluation of the reliability of current information is crucial in developing new applications.	within 2 years
Best-practice approaches to characterize, communicate, and incorporate scientific uncertainty in decisionmaking.	Improvements in how scientific uncertainty is evaluated and communicated can help reduce misunderstanding and misuse of this information.	within 2 years
Decision support experiments and evaluations using seasonal to interannual forecasts and observational data.	Climate variability is an important factor in resource planning and management; improved application of forecasts and data can benefit society.	within 2 years

ATMOSPHERIC COMPOSITION
CLIMATE VARIABILITY AND CHANGE
GLOBAL WATER CYCLE
LAND-USE/LAND-COVER CHANGE
GLOBAL CARBON CYCLE
ECOSYSTEMS
HUMAN CONTRIBUTIONS AND RESPONSES

Land-Use/Land-Cover Change

Land cover refers to everything covering the land surface, including vegetation, bare soil, buildings and infrastructure, inland bodies of water, and wetlands. Land use refers to societal arrangements and activities that affect land cover. Land cover and use influence climate and weather at local to global scales; they can have direct impacts on climate by affecting the composition of the atmosphere and the exchange of energy between continents and the atmosphere. Because of this, land-cover characteristics are key inputs to climate models. Land cover and use also affect water runoff, the carbon and nitrogen cycles, and the distribution of plants and animals in ecosystems.

CCSP-supported research on land-use/land-cover change focuses on processes that determine changes in land cover and land use at local, regional, and global scales; and on how land cover and use will change over timescales of 10-50 years. Research will quantify the human influences on the land; improve monitoring, measuring, and mapping; and develop projections of changes in land cover and land use based on

assumptions about climate, demographic, economic, and technological trends.

Benefits from this research include:

• Identifying areas of rapid land-use and land-cover change and the extent and impact of major disturbances such as fire, insects, drought, and flooding on land use and land cover

• Identifying past and projected trends in land cover or

land use that are attributable to changes in climate (e.g., changes in forest types, forest margins, agriculture, and desert margins), and identifying U.S. regions where climate change may have the greatest implications for land management

• Identifying the effects of land use and land cover on carbon dynamics and the mitigation and management of greenhouse gases.

Deforestation near Rio Branco, Brazil. Systematic cutting of the forest vegetation starts along roads and then fans out to create the "fishbone" pattern evident in this image. A plume of smoke also is visible. The photo, taken on 28 July 2000 by the satellite-based Multi-angle Imaging SpectroRadiometer's (MISR) vertical-viewing (nadir) camera, covers an area of 336 x 333 kilometers (207 x 209 miles). Source: NASA.

Core Approaches

The CCSP will employ four core approaches in working toward its goals.

1. Scientific Research

Plan, Sponsor, and Conduct Research on Changes in Climate and Related Systems

The greatest percentage of future CCSP budgets will be devoted to continuing this essential investment in scientific knowledge, facilitating the discovery of the unexpected, and advancing the frontiers of research. The CCSP participating agencies will coordinate their work through seven "research elements" that focus on features that make the Earth unique (see Research Element descriptions in text boxes throughout the Vision Document for more information). These features include diverse forms of carbon-based life, water in multiple interacting phases, an oxidizing and protective atmosphere, and a climate system that redistributes energy to make a habitable planet. The seven research elements have evolved from the framework for research presented in *Global Environmental Change: Research Pathways for the Next Decade*, a report from the National Research Council that lays out advances in knowledge needed to improve predictive capability in Earth systems science:

- **Atmospheric Composition:** How the composition of the global atmosphere is altered by human activities and natural phenomena, and how such changes influence climate, ozone, ultraviolet radiation, pollutant exposure, ecosystems, and human health
- **Climate Variability and Change**: How climate elements that are particularly important to human and natural systems — especially temperature, precipitation, clouds, winds, and storminess — are affected by natural processes and human activities

- **Global Water Cycle:** How natural processes and humans influence the distribution and quality of water, whether changes are predictable, and how variability and change in the water cycle may affect human and natural systems
- **Land-Use/Land-Cover Change:** How changes in land use and land cover interact with atmospheric composition, the global water cycle, biogeochemistry, ecosystems, climate, and socioeconomic factors, and the extent to which land-use and land-cover change are predictable
- **Global Carbon Cycle**: A focus on identifying the size and variability of, and potential future changes to, the Earth's reservoirs and fluxes of carbon, and providing the scientific underpinning for evaluating carbon sequestration opportunities and alternative response options
- **Ecosystems:** How natural and human-induced changes in the environment interact to affect the structure, functioning, and services of ecosystems, and what options society may have to ensure that desirable ecosystem goods and services will be sustained or enhanced
- **Human Contributions and Responses:** How human activities interact to drive changes in the climate system, land use, and related systems, and how humans prepare for and respond to these changes.

In its sponsorship and conduct of research, the CCSP will establish a balance between focus and breadth by involving both decisionmakers and the science community. The program also will encourage integration among research elements to facilitate progress on research topics that span these research areas. This also will help develop knowledge of the evolution of the integrated Earth system, which is strongly affected by numerous interactions among its components at multiple scales. The CCSP will integrate activities such as modeling, observations, and data management in its

ATMOSPHERIC COMPOSITION
CLIMATE VARIABILITY AND CHANGE
GLOBAL WATER CYCLE
LAND-USE/LAND-COVER CHANGE
GLOBAL CARBON CYCLE
ECOSYSTEMS
HUMAN CONTRIBUTIONS AND RESPONSES

Global Carbon Cycle

Carbon is important as one of the building blocks for the food and fiber that sustain human populations, as the primary energy source fueling economies, and as a major contributor to the greenhouse effect and climate change. Carbon dioxide and methane concentrations have been increasing in the atmosphere, primarily as a result of human use of fossil fuels and land.

CCSP-supported research on the global carbon cycle focuses on identifying potential future changes to atmospheric, terrestrial, and oceanic storage of carbon, and movement of carbon among those pools. The program also provides the scientific underpinning for managing carbon sources and sinks. Specific programs and projects focus on North American and oceanic carbon sources and sinks; the impact of land-use change and resource management practices on carbon sources and sinks; projecting future atmospheric carbon dioxide and methane concentrations and changes in land-based and marine carbon sinks; and the global distribution of carbon sources and sinks and how they are changing.

Benefits from this research include:
- Increased understanding of the sources and sinks for carbon, helping to evaluate carbon sequestration strategies and alternative response options
- Improved confidence in projections of atmospheric concentrations of carbon-based greenhouse gases.

Monitoring Carbon Flows. Scientists near Pt. Barrow, Alaska, check instruments that measure fluxes of carbon to and from the atmosphere. Source: Gary Braasch.

research activities. The program will also encourage integration between and among agencies that conduct its scientific programs and supporting activities.

Scientific progress depends on models, which are essential tools for synthesizing observations, theory, and experimental results to investigate how the Earth system works and how it may be affected by human activities. The CCSP will improve the scientific basis of climate and climate impact models, improve modeling infrastructure and capacity, and coordinate and accelerate the use of models to provide information for decisions.

2. Observations

Enhance Observations and Data Management Systems to Generate a Comprehensive Set of Variables Needed for Climate-Related Research

Since the early years of the USGCRP, an expanded program of global observations has been developed to characterize climate variability and change on a global and regional basis. These observations have included paleoclimatic records spanning thousands of years, satellite remote-sensing systems covering the entire globe, and numerous *in situ* observations on land (including the polar regions), in the atmosphere, and throughout the ocean. The suite of available observations includes long-term observations associated with NOAA's satellite monitoring program and global weather observations, which have not historically been considered as part of the USGCRP; several long-term surface-based measurement networks operated by NASA, NOAA, DOE, and other agencies; and several long-running NASA research satellites and series of satellites, as well as a large number of limited-duration measurements obtained during research campaigns.

Prior and current investments in new observations, as they come to fruition, will significantly enhance knowledge of environmental variables in the coming years. But there is also a need for enhanced global and regional integration of observation and data management systems, especially to help generate new and improved products for supporting decisions. The CCSP will expand the capacity to prioritize, ensure the quality of, archive, and disseminate (in useful format) the large quantity of available observations.

The CCSP will develop new requirements for observation systems to support integrated evaluation of climate and ecosystem parameters. Improved observation systems will address additional research issues, including those having to do with ecosystems, with changes in land use or land cover, and with feedbacks among climate variables.

In implementing its observing strategy, the CCSP will adhere to NRC climate monitoring principles, as well as to the Global Climate Observing System (GCOS) climate monitoring principles for satellites. The program will also seek to foster closer integration of – and cooperation among – research and operational activities and programs. The CCSP will improve strategies for the transition of observational systems originally developed for research to an operational setting in order to carry out long-term monitoring and data collection. The program will benefit from, and contribute to, the design and operational implementation of a new international Earth Observation program. The program, initiated at a meeting hosted by the U.S. Government in July 2003, will be developed over the next 10 years.

3. Decision Support

Develop Improved Science-Based Resources to Aid Decisionmaking

The available scientific record has been used for many years to address a range of questions, from detecting climate change and attributing it to particular causes, to utilizing satellite and ground-based observations and related analyses in

ATMOSPHERIC COMPOSITION
CLIMATE VARIABILITY AND CHANGE
GLOBAL WATER CYCLE
LAND-USE/LAND-COVER CHANGE
GLOBAL CARBON CYCLE
ECOSYSTEMS
HUMAN CONTRIBUTIONS AND RESPONSES

Ecosystems

Ecosystems shape our societies and nations by providing essential renewable resources and other benefits including food, fiber, timber, energy, biodiversity, clean air and water, and non-material (e.g., aesthetic) values. Their capacity to provide such benefits is affected by climate variability and change, and by human influences. Improving projections of future climate and global changes depends on improved understanding of ecosystem processes under multiple natural and human influences.

Research on ecosystems conducted and supported by Federal agencies under the CCSP focuses on how natural and human-induced changes in the environment interact to affect the structure, functioning, and services of ecosystems – including those ecosystem processes that in turn influence regional and global environmental changes. Research also focuses on what options society may have to ensure that ecosystem goods and services are sustained or enhanced. Specific focus areas include key processes that link ecosystems with climate; consequences of global change for ecosystems at different

scales; and options for managing agricultural lands, forests, and other ecosystems.

Benefits from this research include:
• Quantification of important feedbacks from ecological systems to climate and atmospheric composition to improve the accuracy of climate projections
• Updated information on the

sensitivity and adaptability of key ecosystems to climate variability and change, including the potential for abrupt change
• Comprehensive indicators of ecosystem change and health
• Information to support management decisions for agricultural lands, forests, fisheries, and other ecosystems under conditions of environmental change.

Elevated CO$_2$ Concentration Experiment. The Smithsonian Environmental Research Center (SERC) is conducting a series of innovative experiments that expose portions of salt marsh and forest ecosystems to elevated CO$_2$ concentrations in outdoor chambers. Source: Smithsonian Environmental Research Center.

resource management applications. The CCSP will improve interactions with stakeholders and develop resources to support public discussion and planning, adaptive management, and policymaking. It also will encourage development of new methods, models, and other resources that facilitate economic analysis, decisionmaking under conditions of uncertainty, and integration and interpretation of information from the natural and social sciences in particular decision contexts.

Evaluation and communication of uncertainty and levels of confidence is crucial to supporting decisions. CCSP research will address fundamental uncertainties. However, uncertainty can never be completely eliminated, and thus it is also important to develop approaches for using scientific information in decisions made when there are substantial uncertainties. This will help decisionmakers understand the uses and limits of the available information. The CCSP will develop and employ transparent and systematic approaches for decision support, and will evaluate, quantify, and report levels of confidence and uncertainty.

4. Communications

Communicate Results to Domestic and International Scientific and Stakeholder Communities, Stressing Openness and Transparency

Global climate change is complex and often subject to disputed interpretations even among scientists. Because of the unique, large commitment of public resources to CCSP activities, the CCSP has a responsibility to communicate with interested partners in the United States and throughout the world, and to learn from these partners on a continuing basis. As an essential part of its mission, the CCSP undertakes the significant responsibility of enhancing the quality of public discussion by stressing openness and transparency in its findings and reports.

The CCSP will employ four methods to ensure the trustworthiness of its reported findings:

- Use of structured analyses (usually question-based) for CCSP scientific synthesis, assessment, and projection reports
- Use of transparent methodologies that openly report all key assumptions, methods, data, and uncertainties
- Continuous use of web-based and other forms of information dissemination so that CCSP information is freely available to all interested users
- Frequent use of "draft for comment" methods to seek external review before completion of each key document.

The CCSP also will continue to urge all of its sponsored researchers to seek publication of their findings in the peer-reviewed scientific literature.

Each of these approaches is essential for achieving the CCSP's goals. Scientific Research and Observations will rely heavily on existing programs and mechanisms, as well as integration of capabilities developed outside the prior global change research framework. Decision Support and Communications will require the development of new capabilities and initiatives during the coming years, as well as interactions with other Committee on Environment and Natural Resources and National Science and Technology Council committees.

ATMOSPHERIC COMPOSITION
CLIMATE VARIABILITY AND CHANGE
GLOBAL WATER CYCLE
LAND-USE/LAND-COVER CHANGE
GLOBAL CARBON CYCLE
ECOSYSTEMS
HUMAN CONTRIBUTIONS AND RESPONSES

Human Contributions and Responses

Human activities are an important influence on the global environment. Human responses, through adaptation and mitigation, will strongly influence the social impacts (both positive and negative) of global environmental changes.

CCSP-supported research on human contributions and responses to global change focuses on the interactions of changes in the global environment and human activities. The current focus of this research is on the extent of human influences on the climate system, land use, and on other global environmental changes; analyses of societal sensitivity and adaptability to global environmental change; decisionmaking under conditions of significant complexity and uncertainty; methods for integrating information on climate change and potential response options; and the potential effects of climate variability and change on human health and welfare.

Benefits from these research efforts include:

*   Scenarios strengthened by an improved understanding of the interdependence among economics, population growth, energy consumption, advancements in technologies, and emissions
*   Adaptation strategies to effectively manage the impacts of seasonal and year-to-year climate variability such as El Niño events
*   Elevation maps depicting areas vulnerable to sea level rise and planning maps depicting how state and local governments plan to respond to sea level rise
*   Strategies for communicating climate-related information to resource managers (e.g., farmers, forest landowners, drought policy planners, water utilities) and urban planners at local to national levels
*   Assessments of the potential consequences of global change for human health in the United States.

The Human Influence. Mahantango Creek watershed near Klingerstown, Pennsylvania. Human activities play an important part in many natural systems and are forces for change in the environment at local, regional, and even global scales.

CCSP Organization and Management

The CCSP integrates research on global change and climate change sponsored by its participating agencies and departments. By leveraging the complementary strengths of these agencies and departments, the CCSP facilitates research and applications that would otherwise fall beyond the capabilities of any individual participating agency. The President created the CCSP in February 2002 as part of a new cabinet-level management structure to oversee public investments in climate change science and technology. The new structure also includes the CCTP, which is responsible for accelerating climate change-related technology research and development.

The CCSP approach to management integrates the planning and implementation of the individual climate and global change research programs of the participating federal departments and agencies to reduce overlaps, identify and fill programmatic gaps, and add integrative value to products and deliverables produced under the CCSP's auspices.

Five mechanisms are used to achieve this management approach:
- Executive direction by the cabinet-based management structure, including priority setting, management review, and accountability
- Program implementation by CCSP participating agencies
- Coordinated planning and program implementation through interagency working groups
- External interactions for guidance, evaluation, and feedback
- Coordination and management support from an interagency office accountable to the CCSP interagency governing committee.

Interactions among those responsible for these five management elements are critical for improving the scientific planning, the effectiveness of interagency management, and the focus of climate and global change research to support governmental and non-governmental needs.

About the CCSP Strategic Plan

This Vision Document provides an overview of the CCSP Strategic Plan. The plan describes a strategy for developing knowledge of variability and change in climate and related environmental and human systems, and for encouraging the application of this knowledge. The strategy seeks to optimize the benefits of research that is conducted, sponsored, or applied by 13 agencies and departments of the U.S. Government. The strategy describes in greater detail the goals of the CCSP and its component programs, the products that are expected to result, and the approaches and criteria that will be adopted to implement the program. The table of contents of the Plan is reproduced as Appendix A.

Appendix A

Table of Contents for the CCSP Strategic Plan

The full text of the CCSP Strategic Plan is available at <http://www.climatescience.gov/>.

Appendix B

Principal Areas of Focus for the CCSP Agencies

DEPARTMENT OF AGRICULTURE (USDA)

USDA-sponsored research supports long-term studies to improve our understanding of the roles that terrestrial systems play in influencing climate change, and the potential effects of global change (including water balance, atmospheric deposition, vegetative quality, and ultraviolet-B radiation) on food, fiber, and forestry production in agricultural, forest, and range ecosystems. USDA's research program is strengthening efforts to determine the significance of terrestrial systems in the global carbon cycle, and to identify agricultural and forestry activities that can contribute to a reduction in greenhouse gas concentrations. USDA's research agencies will support the Department in responding to the President's directive to develop accounting rules and guidelines for carbon sequestration projects. Contributions from USDA's research program include the development of improved emission and sequestration coefficients, new tools for accurately measuring carbon and other greenhouse gases, and the development of improved sequestration methodologies.

DEPARTMENT OF COMMERCE (DOC)

The DOC's National Oceanic and Atmospheric Administation (NOAA) mission is: "To understand and predict changes in the Earth's environment and conserve and manage coastal and marine resources to meet the nation's economic, social, and environmental needs. The long-term global change efforts of NOAA are designed to develop a predictive understanding of variability and change in the global climate system, and to advance the application of this information in climate-sensitive sectors through a suite of process research, observations and modeling, and application and assessment activities. Specifically, NOAA's research program includes ongoing efforts in operational *in situ* and satellite observations with an emphasis on oceanic and atmospheric dynamics, circulation, and chemistry; understanding and predicting ocean-land-atmosphere interactions, the global water cycle, and the role of global transfers of carbon dioxide among the atmosphere, ocean, and terrestrial biosphere in climate change; improvements in climate modeling, prediction, and information management capabilities; the projection and assessment of variability across multiple time scales; the study of the relationship between the natural climate system and society and the development of methodologies for applying climate information to problems of social and economic consequences; and archiving, managing, and disseminating data and information useful for global change research. DOC's National Institute of Standards and Technology (NIST) provides measurements and standards that support accurate and reliable climate observations. NIST also performs calibrations and special tests of a wide range of instruments and measurement techniques for accurate measurements. NIST provides a wide array of data and modeling tools that provide key support to developers and users of complex climate prediction models.

DEPARTMENT OF DEFENSE (DOD)

The Department of Defense does not support dedicated global change research, but continues a history of participation in the CCSP through sponsored research that concurrently satisfies national security requirements and stated goals of the CCSP. All data and research results are routinely made available to the civil science community. DOD science and technology investments are coordinated and reviewed through the Defense Reliance process and published annually in the Defense Science and Technology Strategy, the Basic Research Plan, the Defense Technology Area Research Plan, and the Joint Warfighting Science and Technology Plan.

DEPARTMENT OF ENERGY (DOE)

Research supported by DOE's Office of Biological and Environmental Research (BER) is focused on the effects of energy production and use on the global Earth system, primarily through studies of climate response. Research includes climate modeling, aerosol and cloud properties and processes affecting the Earth's radiation balance, and sources and sinks of energy-related greenhouse gases (primarily carbon dioxide). It also includes research on the consequences of climatic and atmospheric changes for ecological systems and resources, the development of improved methods and models for conducting integrated economic and environmental assessments of climate change and of options for mitigating climate change, and education and training of scientists for climate change research.

DEPARTMENT OF HEALTH AND HUMAN SERVICES (HHS)

Four National Institutes of Health (NIH) institutes support research on the health effects of ultraviolet (UV) and near-UV radiation. Their principal objectives include an increased understanding of the effects of UV and near-UV radiation exposure on target organs (e.g., eyes, skin, immune system) and of the molecular changes that lead to these effects, and the development of strategies to prevent the initiation or promotion of disease before it is clinically defined. In addition, the National Institute of Environmental Health Sciences (NIEHS) supports research on the health effects of chlorofluorocarbon replacement chemicals, including studies on the metabolism and toxicity of hydrofluorocarbons and halogenated hydrocarbons. HHS (NIH and the Centers for Disease Control and Prevention) also conducts research related to other impacts of global change on human health, including renewed concern about infectious diseases whose

incidence could be affected by environmental change. In addition, NIH sponsors a program to assess the impact of population change on the physical environment and to account for effects of the physical environment on population change.

DEPARTMENT OF THE INTERIOR (DOI)

Research at DOI's U.S. Geological Survey (USGS) contributes directly to the CCSP's intellectual framework of a whole-system understanding of global change (i.e., the interrelationships among climate, ecological systems, and human behavior). The USGS examines terrestrial and marine processes and the natural history of global change, including the interactions between climate and the hydrologic system. Studies seek to understand the character of past and present environments and the geological, biological, hydrological, and geochemical processes involved in environmental change. The USGS supports a broad area of global change research, with a focus on understanding the sensitivity of natural systems and impacts of climate change and variability, surficial processes, and other global change phenomena on the nation's lands and environments at the regional scale. Specific goals of the program are: to improve the utility of global change research results to land management agencies; to emphasize monitoring the landscape and developing technical approaches to identifying and analyzing changes that will take advantage of a burgeoning archive of remotely sensed and *in situ* data; and to emphasize the response of biogeographic regions and features, particularly montane, coastal, and inland wetland ecosystems.

DEPARTMENT OF STATE (DOS)

Through DOS annual funding, the United States is the world's leading financial contributor to the United Nations Framework Convention on Climate Change and to the Intergovernmental Panel on Climate Change, a major organization for the assessment of scientific, technical, and socioeconomic information relevant to the understanding of climate change, its potential impacts, and options for adaptation and mitigation. Recent DOS contributions to the IPCC provide substantial support for the Global Climate Observing System, among other activities.

DEPARTMENT OF TRANSPORTATION (DOT)

DOT utilizes existing science to improve decisionmaking tools in three primary areas: (1) impact of climate variability and change on transportation (research to examine the effects that climate change and variability may have on transportation infrastructure and services, and to identify potential adaptation strategies for use by transportation decisionmakers, operators, state and local planners, and infrastructure builders); (2) increasing energy efficiency and reducing greenhouse gases (research on reducing energy use will cover mitigation of transportation's environmental impacts both through conservation and through the application of new technology); and (3) modeling (research to develop and improve analytical tools for transportation energy use to support decisionmaking throughout government and in the private sector).

AGENCY FOR INTERNATIONAL DEVELOPMENT (USAID)

USAID provides decisionmakers with the information to effectively respond to drought and food insecurity through the Famine Early Warning System Network (FEWS NET). FEWS NET analyzes remote-sensing data and ground-based meteorological, crop, and rangeland observations to track progress of rainy seasons in semi-arid regions of Africa in order to identify early indications of potential famine.

ENVIRONMENTAL PROTECTION AGENCY (EPA)

EPA's Global Change Research Program is an assessment-oriented program with primary emphasis on understanding the potential consequences of climate variability and change on human health, ecosystems, and socioeconomic systems in the United States. This entails: (1) improving the scientific basis for evaluating effects of global change on air quality, water quality, ecosystems, and human health in the context of other stressors and in light of human dimensions (as humans are catalysts of and respond to global change); (2) conducting assessments of the risks and opportunities presented by global change; and (3) assessing adaptation options to increase resiliency to change and improve society's ability to effectively respond to the risks and opportunities presented by global change. EPA's program emphasizes the integration of the concepts, methods, and results of the physical, biological, and social sciences into decision support frameworks.

NATIONAL AERONAUTICS AND SPACE ADMINISTRATION (NASA)

The mission of NASA's Earth Science Enterprise is to understand and protect our home planet by using our view from space to study the Earth system and improve prediction of Earth system change. NASA programs are aimed at understanding the Earth system and applying Earth system science to improve prediction of climate, weather and natural hazards in partnership with other Federal agencies and international space and research programs. Its Research Strategy orchestrates observing and modeling programs to address these essential questions:

- How is the Earth changing, and what are the consequences for life on Earth?
- How is the global Earth system changing?
- What are the primary causes of change in the Earth system?
- How does the Earth system respond to natural and human-induced change?

- What are the consequences of change in the Earth system for human civilization?
- How well can we predict future changes in the Earth system?

NASA's portfolio includes observations, research, analysis, modeling, and advanced technology development, in order to answer selected science questions, and benchmarking decision support resources to ensure society receives the benefits of this research.

NATIONAL SCIENCE FOUNDATION (NSF)

NSF programs address global change issues through investments in challenging ideas, creative people, and effective tools. In particular, NSF global change research programs support research and related activities to advance the fundamental understanding of physical, chemical, biological, and human systems and the interactions among them. The programs encourage interdisciplinary activities and focus particularly on Earth system processes and the consequences of change. NSF programs facilitate data acquisition and information management activities necessary for fundamental research on global change, and promote the enhancement of models designed to improve understanding of Earth system processes and interactions and to develop advanced analytic methods to facilitate basic research. NSF also supports fundamental research on the general processes used by organizations to identify and evaluate policies for mitigation, adaptation, and other responses to the challenge of varying environmental conditions.

SMITHSONIAN INSTITUTION

Within the Smithsonian Institution, global change research is conducted at the Smithsonian Astrophysical Observatory, the National Air and Space Museum, the Smithsonian Environmental Research Center, the National Museum of Natural History, the Smithsonian Tropical Research Institute, and the National Zoological Park. Research is organized around themes of atmospheric processes, ecosystem dynamics, observing natural and anthropogenic environmental change on daily to decadal time scales, and defining longer term climate proxies present in the historical artifacts and records of the museums as well as in the geologic record at field sites. The Smithsonian Institution program strives to improve knowledge of the natural processes involved in global climate change, provide a long-term repository of climate-relevant research materials for present and future studies, and to bring this knowledge to various audiences, ranging from scholarly to the lay public. The unique contribution of the Smithsonian Institution is a long-term perspective – for example, undertaking investigations that may require extended study before producing useful results and conducting observations on sufficiently long (e.g., decadal) time scales to resolve human-caused modification of natural variability.

Appendix C

Key Gaps in the Science of Climate Change

From the White House document at:
<http://www.whitehouse.gov/news/releases/2001/06/climatechange.pdf>
"Advancing the Science of Climate Change"
Key Gaps in Science of Climate Change

Despite major investments in climate change science by the United States and other nations over the past decade, and despite major accomplishments by scientists throughout the world, numerous gaps remain in our understanding of climate change. The National Academy of Sciences identified in its report, *Climate Change Science: An Analysis of Some Key Questions* (June 2001), critical uncertainties about the science of climate change. Fundamentally, the report indicated the need to better understand the causes of warming. The National Academy of Sciences stated, "Greenhouse gases are accumulating in Earth's atmosphere as a result of human activities, causing surface air temperatures and subsurface ocean temperatures to rise. Temperatures are, in fact, rising. The changes observed over the last several decades are likely mostly due to human activities, but we cannot rule out that some significant part of these changes is also a reflection of natural variability."

The National Academy of Sciences report goes on to identify a range of specific areas that require additional study and research. The following considerations provide important information that will be used in setting priorities:

How much carbon is sequestered by oceans and terrestrial sinks and how much remains in the atmosphere is uncertain:
- "How land contributes, by location and processes, to exchanges of carbon with the atmosphere is still highly uncertain… " (p. 11)
- "These estimates [of future carbon dioxide climate forcings]… are only approximate because of uncertainty about how efficiently the ocean and terrestrial biosphere will sequester atmospheric CO_2." (p. 13)
- "How much of the carbon from future use of fossil fuels will be seen as increases in carbon dioxide in the atmosphere will depend on what fractions are taken up by land and by the oceans. The exchanges with land occur on various time scales, out to centuries for soil decomposition in high latitudes, and they are sensitive to climate change. Their projection into the future is highly problematic." (p. 18)

The feedbacks in the climate system that determine the magnitude and rate of temperature increases are uncertain:
- "Because there is considerable uncertainty in current understanding of how the climate system varies naturally and reacts to emissions of greenhouse gases and aerosols, current estimates of the magnitude of future warming should be regarded as tentative and subject to future adjustments (either upward or downward)." (p. 1)
- "Much of the difference in predictions of global warming by various climate models is attributable to the fact that each model represents these [feedback] processes in its own particular way. These uncertainties will remain until a more fundamental understanding of the processes that control atmospheric relative humidity and clouds is achieved." (p. 4)

The direct and indirect effects of aerosols are uncertain:
- "The greatest uncertainty about the aerosol climate forcing—indeed, the largest of all the uncertainties about global climate forcings—is probably the indirect effect of aerosols on clouds." (p. 14)
- "The great uncertainty about this indirect aerosol climate forcing presents a severe handicap both for the interpretation of past climate change and for future assessments of climate changes." (p. 14)
- "Climate forcing by anthropogenic aerosols is a large source of uncertainty about future climate change." (p. 13)
- "Because of the scientific uncertainties associated with the sources and composition of carbonaceous aerosols, projections of future impacts on climate are difficult." (p. 12)

The details and impacts of regional climate change resulting from global climate change are uncertain:
- "On the regional scale and in the longer term, there is much more uncertainty" with respect to effects on agriculture and forestry. (p. 19)
- "The Northern Hemisphere as a whole experienced a slight cooling from 1946-75, and the cooling during that period was quite marked over the eastern United States. The cause of this hiatus in the warming is still under debate." (p. 16)
- "Health outcomes in response to climate change are the subject of intense debate…The understanding of the relationships between weather/climate and human health is in its infancy and therefore the health consequences of climate change are poorly understood. The costs, benefits, and availability of resources for adaptation are also uncertain." (p. 20)
- "Changes in storm frequency and intensity are one of the more uncertain elements of future climate change prediction." (p. 20)

The nature and causes of the natural variability of climate and its interactions with forced changes are uncertain:

- "Because of the large and still uncertain level of natural variability inherent in the climate record and the uncertainties in the time histories of the various forcing agents (and particularly aerosols), a causal linkage between the buildup of greenhouse gases in the atmosphere and the observed climate changes during the 20th century cannot be unequivocally established." (p. 17)
- "The value of indirect effect of ozone changes induced by solar ultraviolet irradiance variations "remains highly uncertain." (p. 14)

The future usage of fossil fuels and the future emissions of methane are uncertain:

- "With a better understanding of the sources and sinks of methane, it may be possible to encourage practices...that lead to a decrease in atmospheric methane and significantly reduce future climate change." (p. 13)
- "There is no definitive scientific basis for choosing among several possible explanations for these variations in the rates of change of global methane contributions, making it very difficult to predict its future atmospheric concentrations." (p. 11)

In response to these gaps in our knowledge, the National Academy of Sciences study also recommends, "research that couples physical, chemical, biological, and human systems; an improved capability of integrating scientific knowledge, including its uncertainty, into effective decision support systems, and an ability to conduct research at the regional or sectoral level that promotes analysis of the response of human and natural systems to multiple stresses."

The NAS report also indicates that to advance the understanding of climate change, it will be necessary to have "a global observing system in support of long-term climate monitoring and prediction [and] concentration on large-scale modeling through increased, dedicated supercomputing and human resources." High priority areas for further research also are identified in numerous recent reports and documents, such as: *Global Environmental Change: Research Pathways for the Next Decade* (1999), *Capacity of U.S. Climate Modeling to Support Climate Change Assessment Activities* (1998), *Adequacy of Climate Observing Systems* (1999), and others.

CLIMATE CHANGE SCIENCE PROGRAM OFFICE

James R. Mahoney, CCSP Director

Richard H. Moss, CCSPO Director

David M. Allen

Jeff Amthor

Susan K. Avery

James H. Butler

Margarita Conkright Gregg

David J. Dokken [TECHNICAL EDITOR]

Susanna Eden

Genene Fisher

Stephanie A. Harrington

Chester J. Koblinsky

David M. Legler

Sandy MacCracken

Jessica Orrego

Rick S. Piltz

Nicholas A. Sundt

Ahsha N. Tribble

Bud Ward

Robert C. Worrest

To obtain a copy of this document, contact:

Climate Change Science Program Office
1717 Pennsylvania Avenue, NW
Suite 250
Washington, DC 20006
202-223-6262 (voice)
202-223-3065 (fax)
information@climatescience.gov
http://www.climatescience.gov/
http://www.usgcrp.gov/

The Climate Change Science Program
incorporates the U.S. Global Change
Research Program and the Climate Change
Research Initiative.

www.ingramcontent.com/pod-product-compliance
Lightning Source LLC
Chambersburg PA
CBHW081408170526
45166CB00010B/3259